Disclaimer

The content of this book is completely believed to be accurate by the author at the date that it was published. The author, publishers or others involved cannot accept legal responsibility for any missing parts or errors made. There is no warranty with respect of the material herein. No parts of the book may be copied and/or published without the expressed written consent of the author.

ISBN-13:

978-1986610605

ISBN-10:

1986610608

Foreword:

I wrote this book so young kids could learn coding easily with the click of a button, a big part of the Information Age, and so that they could express their creativity. Python grants that and more. It gives them knowledge about logic, and puzzles their minds, making them want to know more and expand. This book includes an answer sheet for the quizzes and tests inside. There are a couple pages of projects that you or your child may want to go over.

There are Beginners, with no knowledge, Advanced, with much knowledge, and Intermediate, somewhere in the middle. As the book progresses, you or your child will learn so that they can move up and code bigger programs, which soon turn in to apps, small websites, and then a big business like Apple™. Thank you for reading this book, and I hope you got what you were looking for!

```
print("Happy Coding!!")
```

- Ryan Ghorishy, Author

PART 1:

THE MAJORITY

Chapter 1: BEGINNERS

Python is a coding language. Code is just instructions for the computer to follow. It is very easy to download, as all you need to do is go to www.python.org/downloads and click "Download Python 3.6.4." After Python has downloaded, you are easily on your way to become a coding master and wow your friends.

As a beginner, you have little or no experience, so this section will be easy, just learning the basics. First, let's start with what you see when you open the application. A small rectangle should appear, along with some information at the top. If you type anything, it should appear on the box, like a document. Try typing a few words, and after each word, press enter. You should get a message in red, saying something along the lines of Traceback (most recent call last): etc.

The first command you should learn is the Print command. Type 'print' in all lowercase and it should turn purple. Print means that you want to make the computer type something. After the word 'print,' put some parentheses. This lets the computer know you want to put some information to print. After typing the parentheses, put double quotes around what you want to type. Notice quotes make the text turn green. Try it with HELLO WORLD. If you did it correct, the next line should be the blue words, HELLO WORLD. In the console, commands are immediately carried out. Since we want to create something bigger, we press ⌘N for Macs, or control+N for the rest, and a new tab should appear, completely empty.

Now if you type a print statement and press enter, nothing happens. When you press F5, two things should happen. It should ask if you would like to save, in which you should say 'yes'. Then it will give you a box to name. The stopgap name it gives is Untitled.py, so you can either use that or change the name to remember. You may only have one document that is named anything: the rest must have different names. Then, the first box should reappear and the line will be blue, saying whatever you told it to say.

The next things are the most important parts of Python: variables and data types. A variable is like a box for storing information. Using variables, we can make code shorter. To make a variable, you must do three things. First, type in your variable. There are not supposed to be any spaces, so just use an _ instead. Variables are case sensitive, so try not to use capital letters. Then type an equal sign, then anything you want. If it is a word, put double quotes around the words. Let's make a variable together. Type first_variable into the blank box. Then type an equal sign, then a number. On the next line, type a print statement telling it to print first_variable. Do not put quotes around it, or else the computer will think that you want it to type first_variable and not the number. Keep parentheses on the variable, though. Your code should say something like:

```
first_variable = 4
print(first_variable)
```

When you press F5 to run it, the first box pops up and should print out the number 4. Operators, like +, -, x, ÷, exponents, and modulo (remainder, or the % key) are represented in python as +, -, *, /, **, and %. Using the first two can save time, so you can say ("Hello", first_variable) and get Hello 4. When using strings, you can add them, like "Hello"+"World". You can also add variables, like:

    word = "Hi"

    print(word+word)

The code would give you HiHi

Data types are the four different types of variables. There are floats, signified as float, integers, signified as int, strings, as str, and booleans named bool. Booleans are True or False. Strings are always in quotes. Integers are just numbers, and floats are numbers with a decimal point. You will soon learn how to cast these data types.

Another important thing is called comments. Using the # button marks everything on that line past it red. That means it doesn't affect the code. Let's take the code above:

    print(word+word) #This will not affect the code! I can write whatever I want!
    But now I can't. This affects my code.

To stop this problem, there is a multi-line comment. Use three quote marks, and this happens:

    print(word+word) ''' Now my code won't be affected

    Look! It still is green! To stop the comment, I just add ''' and voila! I am

    affecting the code!

PROJECT 1:

Your first project is to create a program that puts your name in a box,

like this:

```
*****************************************************************************
*                                                                           *
*                                                                           *
*                            Hello, Name!                                   *
*                                                                           *
*****************************************************************************
```

The trick is, you cannot use:

More than one asterisk in the same line:

"**"

"*"

"***"

(The green highlighted area is correct, while the red areas are wrong.)

Or more than one space in the same line:

"   "

" "

"   "

```
print("***")
```

```
print(" * ")
```

```
print(" * ")
```

Use variables! Reread the past pages to get an idea. Answer at the end of the book.

Each project is worth up to 5 points, but you may get 1 point extra credit!

QUIZ

This is a quiz to test your knowledge. There are 4 multiple choice answers, with 5 questions. Set a timer for 4 minutes. No looking back on the previous sections. GO!

1) What color is a print statement?

   a) Red

   b) Blue

   c) Purple

   d) Green

2) What are the rules of making a variable?

   a) Type print, then type the variable

   b) Type the variable name, a subtraction sign, and the thing you want to make the variable

   c) Type the variable name, an equal sign, and what the variable is

   d) None of the above

3) Which of these are a print statement?

   a) print "Hi"

   b) Print ("YO")

   c) ("Yay!")

   d) print ("HO HO HO")

4) What is the definition of code?

a) Cool

b) Python

c) Instructions

d) Computers

5) Name the four data types.

a) Int, Bool, Str

b) Float, Print, Str, Int

c) Variable, Int, Str, Bool

d) Int, Bool, Str, Float

Answers are revealed at the end of the book.

CHAPTER 2: BEGINNER

Now that we can write a bit of code, let's learn about input. As you can see, input turns purple, meaning it is a command. Input (commands, strings, and conditionals are not colorful when a letter, like the 'I' in Input, is capitalized) asks the user for an answer to a question or statement. Input is created by a variable: a = input("Question")It is like a print statement in a couple ways. Let's compare them:

```
question = input("Question")
RESULT:
Question
```

```
print("Question")
RESULT:
Question
```

See? The only difference is that you can answer the first. If you answer it, let's say with YES, question = "YES".

Another couple important things to learn about are if , elif , and else. These are orange, because they are conditional statements. These three things help code programs. The format you use is if, elif, or else , variable, and either ==, >,<, <= (less than or equal to) or >= (greater than or equal to), or even != (not equal to) a

variable/value, and a colon:

```python
if first_variable == 4:

        print(first_variable)

elif first_variable > 4:

        print(first_variable-1)

else:

        print("I don't know")
```

Notice that else does not have anything after. That is because else does not

need another argument. You can have as many elif statements as you want, but

only 1 if or else statement.

Loops are also orange. There are two main types: while and for loops. In

Beginner, we will only talk about while loops. They are formatted a bit like if

statements, with if or while in the front, but for a while loop, it should look like this:

```python
while first_variable == 4:

        print(first_variable)
```

The following code gives you:

4

4

4

And on forever. The reason is because the only way a loop will end is that one of a couple things happen. First, at the end of the loop, you could type the word break. That stops the loop. If you want to make the loop go for a certain amount of times, let's say, 4, you would do this:

```python
while first_variable != 0:
        print(first_variable)
        first_variable = first_variable - 1
```

The code would end up typing:

4

3

2

1

It decreased because the computer sees that first_variable keeps decreasing, so when it gets to zero, the code will stop. The other type of while loop commonly used is a while True loop. There are two major things you should see: the word true is capitalized, and that it is orange. True is a boolean. Booleans are true or false statements. To understand why we use true, you can use a chart:

A	B	not A	not B	A or B	A and B
True	False	False	True	True	False
False	False	True	True	False	False
True	True	False	False	True	True
False	True	False	False	True	False

The chart has three extra conditionals: not, or, and. These do exactly like they sound like: not meaning the opposite of, or meaning that at least one has to be true, and meaning all of them have to be true. Basically, what the chart is saying is, if A is True and B is False, then (A and B) is False, (A or B) is True, and (not A) is False, while (not B) is True.

Casting is a branch of data types that can be very useful, most times about inputting values.

```
A = input("What is your favorite number?")
```

To cast this, we add one of the other data types besides strings.

```
A = int(input("What is your favorite number?"))
```

That changes A from "8" to 8. If we ask for a number, we use either integers or floats. The least common used one is a boolean. It is the hardest one to use since you don't really have many scenarios at the stage we are at for them, except for loops. Notice that for every cast, there is one more parenthese at the end. You can cast multiple times, too:

```
A = int(float(bool(input("This is a boolean!!!!"))))
```

Learning about casting is important in python. Casting is the way to make calculators or any number or True/False statement for, let's say, a poll, you could check to see if the majority of the people want a new highway versus wanting to lower toll costs, or whether they like who the president is or would like another candidate. Casting will help in many of the ahead projects, so you may want to spend a bit more time here before you move on to the next big project, which will include input, while loops, and casting. To get you ready, we will do a quick review.

INPUT: _a command telling the console to ask a user to insert data into a variable. May be casted (See below definition). Example: a = input("What is …")_

WHILE LOOPS: _a conditional where a block of code is repeated over and over until a certain condition or requirement is met. Example: while a == 1:_

CASTING: _a part of most code in python in which an input statement (see above definition) asks the user for the data and changes the data from a string to the data type used in the casting process. Input statements may be casted more than once. Example: a = float(int(input("This is a number"))_

Integers, Floats, Booleans, And Strings: *The four data types. An integer and a float are different because an integer has no decimal point value, while a float, or floating point number, also called doubles, may have a decimal point value. Floats CAN have no decimal point, but integers CANNOT have a decimal point. (The same goes for a square is a rectangle but a rectangle is a square). Examples:*

Int: 32

Bool: True

String: "Hi"

Float: 3.141592

If, Elif, Else: *The three conditional statements.* ***If*** *something is True (See below) then (insert code) happens.* ***Elif*** *it's True for THIS statement, but False for the* ***If*** *statement, (insert different code) happens.* ***Else*** *meaning that if none of the above is True, (insert completely different code) happens. E.g. (if/elif/else) n == 3:*

TRUE/FALSE: *True and False are booleans. They can be casted (see above) into an integer or string, (True = 1, False = 0), and are mostly used in* ***while loops*** *or* ***If/Elif/Else*** *statements (see above). E.g. True*

PROJECT 2:

Learning about input and loops is the way to get this project! What you have to do is create a calculator that can use decimals, addition, subtraction, multiplication, division, and solve for the remainder. There are no restrictions, as long as it can take any two numbers and add them, subtract them, multiply, divide, and give the remainder or solve an exponent. You must use a While loop that runs until the user types "break" (no capitals). The calculator should ask the user:

What the first number is (Use a float)

What the second number is (Use a float)

What operator to use (Reread Ch 1) {+,-,*,/,%,**}

It should answer with the sum, difference, product, remainder, or power. Then it should ask if the computer would like to continue. If they don't they should type "break" without capitals. Good Luck!

Answers at the end of book.

TEST

This is a test. There are 4 multiple choice answers, with 5 questions. Set a timer for 2 minutes. No looking back on the previous sections. GO!

1) What does the color orange represent?

    a) A command

    b) A string

    c) A boolean

    d) A conditional

2) If A is true and B is true, which one of these are true?

    a) Not A

    b) A or B

    c) Not A or B

    d) Not B

3) Which one of these are correctly casted?

    a) A = int(input(bool("YO")))

    b) A = int(bool(input("YO")))

    c) A = float("YO")

    d) A = input("yo")

4) '''Am I affecting the

code?? ''' #How about now?

    a) Yes both times

    b) No and Yes

    c) Yes and No

    d) No both times

5) Name the two types of boolean.

    a) bool, True

    b) False, bool

    c) while True

    d) True, False

Answers are revealed at the end of the book.

1-2: review previous lessons before continuing

3: Skim through previous lessons

4-5: Great Job! Go to the next page.

Chapter Three: Intermediate

Congratulations! You have passed the level of beginners. You are now an intermediate coder, and the chapters are going to get smaller and smaller. You have a bit of experience, and are on your way to becoming the greatest coder on the entire planet of Earth! The next thing we need to learn about is a big thing called a function. To declare a function, you type:

```python
def function_name():
    print("this is what the function does")
function_name()
```

The code is basically defining a function, telling the computer what it does, and then calling the function by name. The code would not do anything if the third line was not there. You need to call your function, using its name and the parentheses. You can add parameters inside the parentheses, like a variable or two:

```python
def function_name2(param1, param2):
    print(param1 + param2)
function_name2(3, 4)
```

This gives you:

```
7
```

Because param1 is 3, according to the third line. The order of the variables is shown in line 1, where param1 is substituted with 3. The same is said about param2.

Since functions are very hard, we'll jump right in to our first project as intermediates.

PROJECT 1:

Using all your knowledge, create a simple program using at least 1 function, named blastoff_timer, one parameter, named user_num, and create a timer that counts down from an inputted number until zero, where it says, "Blastoff!". Use a while loop, and do not use variables.

(HINT: put the while loop in the function so not to get a syntax error)

Try this line of code:

```python
def blastoff_timer(user_num):

    while user_num != 0:
```

GOOD LUCK! It's harder than the beginner projects!

Answers at the back of book

Re-Test

This is a quiz to test your knowledge of the previous three chapters. You have two minutes, and you have to answer each question with at least two sentences.

I.   What is a While Loop?

     Explain

II.   What is a conditional?

      Explain

III.   What colors are in python?

IV.   Cast a boolean with at least two casts

V.   Name the four data types and explain each of them.

VI.   Write a while loop telling the computer to print first_variable (which is 9) 8 times.

Answers at the back of the book.

CHAPTER 4: Intermediate

Now that you have learned all about functions, you can learn what was barely described in chapter two: FOR loops.

These loops are orange, and they are loops used when you have a block of code which you want to repeat a fixed number of times. The for statement writes the code in order, executing the code each time.

To use the loop you must also learn in , range and (x). In is part of a loop, where it is exactly what it sounds like. (X) is a stopgap used in for loops.

Range is just a list from the first number to the number before the last number:

```python
for x in range(1, 100):
    print(x)
```

That would give you a list of numbers from 1 to 99. You can add a third number at the end to skip count.

```python
for x in range(2, 16, 2):
    print(x)
2
4
6
8
10
12
14
```

It skip counted by twos because I wrote 2 after the 16. It also skipped the 16 because Range skips the last number, so 15 is the last number. But since 15 is odd, it went to the nearest even number down: 14. Skip counting is very useful for finding things like factors of a number, or making a fibonacci sequence, or even calculating a factorial.

A big project is coming up, and so is the test. Let's do another review:

RANGE: _A function used in a for loop, takes the first number given and returns all numbers up to the number before the last.Example: for x in range(1, 101):_

FOR: _The loop using the functions range (see above) and in (see below). See above for example. The for statement returns the code, executing it each time until ended._

_IN:_ _another command used in a for loop, completes the loop and activates range function. See above for an example._

_(X):_ _x is a stopgap. It doesn't really mean anything at all, but is vital if creating a basic for loop._

#2: Double Project!

The project for today is a Double. It takes EVERYTHING you learned, as an intermediate or beginner, and makes

''' ONE

BIG

PROJECT'''

For this project, you will make a geometry calculator that can solve the area of a rectangle or triangle. Use functions for both. rect_area and tri_area are the two you should use. Use a loop so that the calculator keeps going forever. Try to make the entire program less than 10 lines long.

Good Luck!

Test Time!

This is the Final Test as an Intermediate. There are 4 questions. Before you begin, please reread the previous two chapters. Give yourself two minutes two take the test. There are three types of questions on this test: Multiple Choice, explain, or answer. Answer problems mean that you type in what the console prints out. For instance,

```
print("HI")
```

You would write HI as the answer. If there is no answer, write "nothing" in quotes.

1. ```
   def add():
       print("1")
   ```

2. Which of these are true? Write true or false under the statement
   a. There are three data types
   b. Booleans are numbers
   c. Floats have decimals

3. Write a print statement saying "Johnny".

4. ```
   for x in range(2, 10, 2):
       print(x)
   ```

Answers revealed at the end

Chapter 5: ADVANCED!

This section is different. There are no quizzes, but a lot more projects. At the very end, you will be tested on EVERYTHING in this book. There is only one main thing you will learn as an advanced coder is the import function, but under it is an umbrella of code. From here on out, the color-code is only shown in examples of code.

Import is something where you take code from another program. Usually, you would import something from a program written already by Python, like turtle.py. If you have noticed when you save a program, it asks you to name it, Untitled.py (.Py) Stands for python, so you can't delete it. Importing programs goes through the simple steps of:

```
import programname
```

All you did was tell the program to open up programname and add all of it to your code. You won't see it, but all of programname's variables and functions are already into your program. Since programname isn't a real program, a short list of all the programs we will cover are: random, sys, time, turtle, and tkinter.

Random is the first and easiest thing you will learn. Basically, random just picks a random thing (integer or string or sometimes boolean) and uses it. This next part is important. You MUST do this when using this format:

```
import random
random_number = random.randrange(1, 10)
```

You should always put the name with a dot after (random. ,programname. , etc) at the start of the function after you import it.

Randrange is the function name that you use to get the random number. It is the only reason you will need this function for a long time. Notice that in parentheses, there are the numbers 1 to 10.

The randrange function takes the first number, and goes up to the second number. (1, 10) would give you 1,2,3,4,5,6,7,8,9, OR 10. The range function gives you all of them, while RANDrange gives you 1 of them.

Remember that with the progression of the book, the chapters get shorter, the subjects get harder, the projects more difficult, and there will not be a lot of describing EVERY function possible.

PROJECT 1:

This is a project. Keep this program, call it Advanced.py , since you will need this program for the rest of your projects. You need to create a game in which the user is trying to guess a number from 1 to 100. Use the random.randrange function, and make a while loop that goes on until they guess the number. When the user guesses a number, respond, "go higher", "go lower", or "You are correct!". When they get it correct, end the loop with the conditional statement break. Use an if statement to see if the number is correct, too high, or too low.

Answer at the end

Part 2

The next program is sys. sys is a program that basically will be used for exiting the program for now. In case you want to know the other things that sys is used for, you can go to docs.python.org/3.5/contents.html . sys is just used mainly for this reason, and because it is better to use than break or ending the code when you have, let's say, a pick your path adventure, and you die.sys helps end the program immediately, which is helpful instead of typing break twice because:

```python
while True:

        while something == True:

                break

        break
```

Without the second break, the code would still go through the loop. With sys, you could use the exit() function,

```python
while True:

        while something == True:

        sys.exit()
```

This immediately ends all the code completely. It is the shortest and easiest of the programs we use, so without further ado, let's jump back into Advanced.py !

Project 2:

Using sys, get the 1-100 game, and get rid of the break and change it to an exit statement, and try to edit out as much code as possible to keep it less than 20 lines long. Use the exit statement twice. Experiment around, play with the code, and shrink it. To make it harder, make sure that you only use TWO different variables and THREE different print statements. That means that you can use the same print statement infinity times, but three different ones max.

Part 3

The third program is the one you will use a lot of times. The program's name is Time. Time is exactly what it sounds like. You will need only one function for the project: sleep. Sleep is a function that pauses the program for *n* seconds. To set the amount of seconds,

import time

time.sleep(2)

For two seconds. Using this will be very useful, as the next project should be easy enough to figure out. You should reread the other two functions to figure out what to do, and we will do a mini project, one that will just include time.

For this mini-project, create a pick your path adventure, where a character goes through an adventure where the user:

Types their name

Chooses yes or no depending on the questions asked by the console

Will either die eventually or make it through the entire game

And the suspense builds up using the sleep function

When you complete the mini, go to the next part.

Review

Let's just review before this next project. We've learned:

Random (randrange())

Sys (exit())

Time (sleep())

So, randrange gets any number from (a to b), exit stops the program immediately, and sleep pauses the feed for (a) seconds. Three questions are below, one for each.

1: Randrange

Would random.randrange(1, 10.5) give:

a) 10

b) 20

c) 11

d) 10.6

2: Exit

Would sys.exit():

a) Kill the program

b) Stop the loop

c) None of the above

3: Sleep

How long would time.sleep(2+1) last?

a) It doesn't work

b) 3 seconds

c) 1 second

d) 3 minutes

Project 3:

Open up a NEW program, named Adv2.py, and use all three of the functions that you have learned so far: randrange(), exit(), and sleep(). Remember: put the program's name before the function, and import them at the very beginning of the program.

What you will be creating is a simple game of rock, paper, scissors. To help, ask the user to pick number 1 for rock, two for paper, and three for scissors, and then use a random number from the computer to do the same thing, then use if statements to make sure who wins. The output should either be:

Scissors beats paper. You won! Play again?

Tie. Play again?

Rock beats scissors. You lost. Play again?

And the same with paper and scissors. Make sure you use "Play again?" at the end. To add suspense, sprinkle sleep(2) functions before the computer picks, and while explaining the game.

Part 4:

Before we learn the next program, we will talk more about the import statement. There are three things that you can learn. The first one is the from statement. From is used in import statements to change or do something, like:

from program import function

The second command is the asterisk, which means all of the functions. It is formatted the same way, but instead of (function) you type *. The third part is (as).

from program import function as anything

Your code just imported (function) and renamed it (anything). All three of the commands do something special: they make (function, anything, or *) not need the program.function. You could just type function:

from random import randrange as randomnum

randomnum(1, 100)

56

Or:

from random import *

randrange(1, 100)

56

There will not be a project about this, but all the next projects will have 2 extra credit points, with 1 of them about using the above strategies consistently.

The major program to learn is called turtle. Turtle is not an animal, just like Python. It is just a drawing program. There are so many commands to learn, but not all of them are listed here. All of the functions and more are listed with what they do at:

docs.python.org/3/library/turtle.html#turtle-methods.

A quick overview on the functions we will go over are:

Pen, Screen, bgcolor, forward, right, backwards, and left.

Pen is the drawing pen, which you will define after you import the program, and defaults as a black triangle.

turtle.Pen()

Notice the word Pen is capitalized. Python is case sensitive, so you MUST use a capital P when using the Pen. To change the shape or color, you type in the parentheses: ("shape", "color"). If you wanted a red circle, you would type in:

my_pen = turtle.Pen("circle","red")

The next function is Screen. Again, you use a capital "S". The Screen is the box where the turtle drawing will be drawn. You use the same format as the Pen, except you cannot define what shape the board/screen or color. You must define both of these for anything else to happen, so make sure you define them early on.

my_screen = turtle.Screen()

To get a certain color on the background, use the bgcolor function:

my_screen.bgcolor("blue")

In case you are wondering, turtle contains almost any color you can think of and more. If there is more than one word in the color, you just type it without a space, like lightblue or LightBlue . You can only use capitals on two-word colors, and only at the start of each word. The next commands, forward, backward, right, and left, are Pen commands, meaning they are commands that you use for the Pen. When you name the variable Pen, you can use the variable as the Pen. In an example:

```
mypen = turtle.Pen()

myscreen = turtle.Screen()

mypen.forward()
```

The parentheses after the four commands are directions. mypen.forward(90) would go 90 pixels up. If you substitute forward with fd(), it still works. This is the same with backwards, back, and bk, right and rt, and left with lt.

Right and left do not move the Pen right or left. Instead, they move the Pen by turning the Pen. Try it with this code:

```
from turtle import *

mypen = Pen()

myscreen = Screen()

while True:

        mypen.fd(50)

        mypen.rt(90)
```

As you will notice when you run it, the code will keep running forever, but will just keep going on and creating a square.

The rest of the lesson will just be different challenges for you to complete. You don't need to write the import part. Just worry on the variables and actual project.

1) Create a box on top of a box on top of a box on…. Etc

Write your code here:

2) Draw a circle (use a while loop)

Write your code here:

3) Draw a circle next to a box (Should look like: O[])

Write your code here:

THE FINAL PROJECT

Congratulations! You just need to complete this project and the test afterwards, and you will have completed the majority of the Handbook.

THE PROJECT IS............................. To make someone.

This project is one that YOU will grade. For you, it must look PERFECT. You need rounded eyes, a smiling mouth, and a correctly formed nose.

Take your time with this one!

THE FINAL TEST

There are 9 questions in this finals exam. The first three are from beginner codes, the second three from intermediate codes, and the last three from advanced codes. Each piece of code has something (maybe more) wrong with it, and you have to debug the code. Just write the error with < or >:

5. a = 12

   print("a")

<quotation marks>

12. print(c)

<Unknown variable: c>

DO NOT go into Python and look at what's wrong by running it. Some of these do not have a problem in the code, but in the logic. Look above at the #5 example. The coder probably wanted it to print 12 because he defined (a) as 12. #12 didn't define c, so it WOULD be a computer error. You have TWO MINUTES to complete this, and the first couple are pretty easy. Don't risk getting one wrong to save time.

Ready, set, go!

```
1.) print("hello)
```

```
2.) input("What is your favorite color?")
```

```
3.) a = intput("What is your favorite color?")
```

```
4.) while true
        print("hi")
```

```
5.) a = True
    b = False
    if a or b is True:
        print("hi")
```

```
6.) a = 1
    if a == 1:
        print("hi")
```

```
else a = 3:

    print("not hi")
```

7.) imort time

```
time sleep(1)
```

8.) import randrange from random

```
a == randrange(1,3)
```

9.) from sys import exit

```
sys.ext()
```

Annnnnd…. Stop the clock! You're done. Check the timer. Did you make it? If not, how many did you do?

PART 2:

The Minority

Introduction

Congratulations! You have completed the hardest part: the actual learning, testing, and graded projects. If this book was school, that test was the finals exam. The rest of this book will just be some things you may want to consider: projects and answers.

Have fun!

PROJECTS PAGES

(Answer key not included)

1)   For your first project you should create a picture of somebody. Just a small person, it only needs a head, body, and two arms and legs. (29 lines or less)

2)   Create a loop printing a random word from a list of three words with a two-second pause in between.

3) Use 5 lines of code to print 6 DIFFERENT things (Not using a while loop)

Answer Key

(By the order of appearance)

(Something along these lines:)

Project 1:

```
star = "*"

print (star * 75)

space = " "

print (space)

print (star + space*73 + star)

greeting = "Hello ryan"

print (space)

print (star + space*32 + greeting + space *31 + star)

print (space)

print (star + space*73 + star)

print (space)

print (star*75)
```

Quiz 1:

1) C

2) C

3) D

4) C

5) D

Project 2:

```python
a = int(input("What is the first number?"))
b = int(input("What is the second number?"))
c = input("What do you want to do? (add, subtract, multiply, or divide? You can also ask for a remainder or find the exponential value by either typing 'exponent' or 'remainder' ")
if c == "add":
    print (a+b)
elif c == "subtract":
    print (a-b)
elif c == "multiply":
    print (a*b)
if c == "divide":
    print (a/b)
```

```
elif c == "exponent":

        print  (a**b)

else:

        print (a%b)
```

Test:

1) D

2) B

3) B

4) D

5) D

Project 3:

```
a = 5

while True:

        if a == 0:

                print ("Blastoff!")

        print (a)

        a = a-1
```

Re-Test: (answers may vary)

1) A while loop is a conditional statement that executes code, repeating over and over

2) A conditional is an orange statement asking something. If, elif, else and while loops are examples of conditionals.

3) Purple, Orange, Red, and Green.

4) A = int(bool("hi")

5) A string has quotes, an integer is a number without a decimal, a float is a number WITH a decimal, and a boolean is a True or False statement.

6) while first_variable != 1:

    print(first_variable)

    first_variable = first_variable - 1

Project 4:

```
def rect_area(a, b):
    print (a * b)
def tri_area(a, b):
    print ((a * b) / 2)
d = input("choose the area of a rectangle or triangle")
if d == "rectangle":
    rect_area(float(input("what is the length?")), float(input("What is the height?")))
```

```
else:

        tri_area(float(input("what is the base length?")), float(input("what is
the height?"))))
```

Test 2:

1) "Nothing"

2) False, False, True

3) print("Johnny")

4) 2, 4, 6, 8

Project 5:

```
import random

b = random.randrange(1, 101)

while True:

        a = int(input("Pick a number from one to one hundred"))

        if a == b:

                print("You win!")

                break

        elif a > b:

                print("Go lower!")

        else:

                print("Go higher!")
```

Project 6:

```
import random
Import sys
b = random.randrange(1, 101)
while True:
        a = int(input("Pick a number from one to one hundred. To quit, type quit"))
        if a == "quit":
                sys.exit()
        elif a == b:
                print("You win!")
                sys.exit()
        elif a > b:
                print("Go lower!")
        else:
                print("Go higher!")
```

Project 7:

```python
import random

import time

import sys

print("This is a game of rock, paper, scissors")

time.sleep(2)

while True:

        a = input("1=rock 2=scissors, 3=paper. to quit, type exit")

        time.sleep(2)

        b = random.randrange(1, 3)

        if a == "exit":

                sys.exit()

        if a == b:

                print("You tied. Try again?")

        elif a == 1 and b == 2:

                print("You win! Try again?")

        elif a == 1 and b == 3:

                print("You lose! Try again?")

        elif a == 2 and b == 1:

                print("You lose! Try again?")

        elif a == 2 and b == 3:

                print("You win! Try again?")
```

```
elif a == 3 and b == 1:

        print("You win! Try again?")

else:

        print("You lose! Try again?")

time.sleep(2)
```

THE FINAL PROJECT

(Put your grade here: /100)

THE FINAL TEST

<No ending quotation marks>

<No variable in input statement>

<Incorrect spelling: intput>

<Capitalize True, need colon EOL 1>

<Unknown statement: is. Instead: (==)>

<Else statement needs 0 conditionals>

<Incorrect spelling: imort. No period between time or sleep found>

<Incorrect placement of "from". Extra equal sign line 2>

<Incorrect spelling: ext>

Author's Note

I just want to thank everybody who has gotten me up to here. My parents, teachers, and little brother have all helped SO MUCH I just cannot describe. I just wish I could keep teaching kids what they need to know. Thank you, and I hope you enjoyed my book!

- Ryan Ghorishy, Author.

For A Kid, By a Kid

Ryan Ghorishy was a 12 year old coder born and raised in Newport Coast, California at the time of publication. He loves reading, playing sports, and fixing problems. He has a 10-year old brother who always gives him competition, and a great team supporting the creation of the book you have now read. Ghorishy went to Newport Coast Elementary for 7 years of his life. He was a GATE student and a major bibliophile. Ryan loves sports and is a true Dallas Cowboys fan.

AfterWord:

I just really appreciate everything that has been going on since I started writing this book. The people who have been so involved in this endeavour every step of the way inspired me to change people's thinking about the "It's too hard" in life. If you have read this book from start to finish, you should be able to see the effort not only I put in, but the effort of a group. Thank you.

--- Ryan Ghorishy

www.ingramcontent.com/pod-product-compliance
Lightning Source LLC
Chambersburg PA
CBHW041432050326
40690CB00002B/513